THEN & NOW

HAGERSTOWN

OPPOSITE: This sketch by Theodore R. Davis is from the September 27, 1862, *Harper's Weekly* and shows Hagerstown during its occupation by rebel forces during the Civil War. The related article stated Hagerstown "is a city of about 4500 inhabitants, contains seven churches and three banks, and is the depot for an extensive grain-growing country." Some of those church spires can be seen in the sketch, including St. John's Lutheran Church on South Potomac Street. The tower was used as a lookout to keep tabs on Confederate troops during the war. (Courtesy Washington County Historical Society.)

THEN & NOW

HAGERSTOWN

Mary H. Rubin

Copyright © 2010 by Mary H. Rubin
ISBN 978-0-7385-8584-0

Library of Congress Control Number: 2009941217

Published by Arcadia Publishing
Charleston SC, Chicago IL, Portsmouth NH, San Francisco CA

Printed in the United States of America

For all general information contact Arcadia Publishing at:
Telephone 843-853-2070
Fax 843-853-0044
E-mail sales@arcadiapublishing.com
For customer service and orders:
Toll-Free 1-888-313-2665

Visit us on the Internet at www.arcadiapublishing.com

ON THE COVER: Taken in December 1935, this image looks east down Washington Street toward the public square. The Hotel Alexander can be seen through the winter sky as well as the town Christmas tree in the middle of the intersection of Washington and Potomac Streets. In those days, traffic ran in both directions on both streets. (Then image courtesy Western Maryland Room, Washington County Free Library; now image courtesy of the author.)

ON THE BACK COVER: This image shows Washington Street leading east at the public square in 1957. The Keystone Restaurant is on the corner behind the sign hanger on the ladder. Once a popular downtown spot, the Keystone later became the site of People's Drug Store and lunch counter. (Courtesy Western Maryland Room, Washington County Free Library.)

CONTENTS

ACKNOWLEDGMENTS

The author would like to gratefully acknowledge everyone who helped make this title possible. Creating a "then and now" book presented an exacting set of challenges to find not only unique images representing Hagerstown's past but also historical images that could be pinpointed to a precise current location for a "now" image. Many images came from the archives of the Western Maryland Room of the Washington County Free Library, and John Frye was as helpful as ever. As the creative process to find workable images continued, Frank Woodring from the *Maryland Cracker Barrel* and the Washington County Historical Society were also extremely forthcoming and very generous in opening their collections to allow the utmost range of sources for this title; the final product is a tribute to their contributions. The author would also like to thank Kay Rubin for ongoing and continuous enthusiastic assistance in helping gather and research information and for many long hours in the car in freezing weather while we debated the best angles for "now" images.

All then images are courtesy of the Western Maryland Room, Washington County Free Library unless otherwise noted. All now images are courtesy of the author.

INTRODUCTION

Often considered by many to be a small, backwoods town out in the wilds of Western Maryland, Hagerstown was once the third largest city in the state of Maryland. The town has undergone a great many changes since Jonathan Hager first came to the region in 1739 and officially founded the settlement he named for his wife as Elizabethtown in 1762. The town lies in the heart of the Cumberland Valley along a north-south route that natives had traveled for centuries. The nearby Potomac River and, later, the National Road served as a venue for east-west travel and a passage early Americans used as a gateway to branching out and settling the West.

The Hagerstown area was a popular hunting ground due to the abundant wildlife. However, residents encountered Native Americans in the early years of settlement and, with the unknown wilderness to the west and the Blue Ridge Mountains to the east, help in case of attack would not be easy to obtain. They learned quickly to be self-reliant and independent. Some of our local place names come, in fact, from native words such as "Antietam," which means swift, flowing water.

Washington County (of which Hagerstown is the county seat) was created on September 6, 1776. Originally part of Frederick County, the new county was named for George Washington, commander-in-chief of the Continental Army. Washington had spent time in the area, and one of our main thoroughfares through downtown, Washington Street, would take its name from the country's first president. Many of our other streets throughout town are also named after other important people in Hagerstown's history.

As the new country continued to grow, Hagerstown became an important stopping point on the route west. Pioneers took Hagerstown Almanacs with them as well as many of the products manufactured in Hagerstown to be sold at western outposts. The opening of rail lines into Hagerstown created an additional boom in growth. Remnants of the huge rail operations in town can still be seen today in the rail lines that almost encircle town. The concept of the rail lines radiating out from town in all directions like spokes on a wheel helped give rise to Hagerstown's nickname of "Hub City."

With its critical location on the North/South border, Hagerstown was heavily involved in the Civil War. The town served as a supply center and staging area throughout the war and was occupied by both Confederate and Union troops on a regular basis as they moved between battlegrounds in Virginia and Pennsylvania. One of the most notable events was the "Ransom of Hagerstown" during 1864. On July 6, 1864, Gen. John McCausland demanded the sum of $20,000 as well as supplies from town for his troops or the town would be destroyed by fire. It was the resourcefulness of town leaders that allowed the demand to be met to save the town.

The movement from small settlement to a booming transportation and industrial center for the entire region left its mark, and some of this imprint is still visible in structures throughout town today. Many styles of architecture have found their way into Hagerstown over the years, from the Georgian splendor of the Governor Hamilton residence to the Victorian— and Beaux Arts—style buildings in the core downtown district. Mansion house areas for the industrial magnates of the late-1800s and early-1900s still exist as well as the downtown row house developments for the workers in the town's booming industries.

It is clear that, over the years, history has certainly cast its fortunes on the town, bringing changes wrought by the Civil War, the railroads, the industry, and the pioneer settlers themselves, who carved a home out of this wilderness land in the early years of our country. At the same time, however, the town is one of the fastest growing and changing areas in the state, and the inevitable changes brought by this growth have sometimes changed the old landscape forever. Sometimes change creeps in—an addition tacked on here, some renovation or restoration there—while at other times, it comes at a gallop, as when a historic structure is torn down or completely repurposed.

However change has occurred, any town wishing to retain a sense of its time and place in history should take care to document what went before as much as possible for future generations. In this retrospective look at Hagerstown, we can see how dramatically some areas have altered over the past two and a half centuries. And yet, if we take the time for careful observation, it is amazing to realize just how much has managed to survive the passing of time. As we shape our future, let us be mindful of how history has helped define us and keep one eye to the past and where we have been, even as we look to the future and where we are going.

CHAPTER 1

THE PUBLIC SQUARE BLOCKS

This is the Hagerstown Public Square as it appeared around 1900, looking north on Potomac Street. D. Ramacciotti's fruit and candy store dominated the left side of the square. Note the overall hustle and bustle of the thriving downtown center. Trolleys rolled down the middle of the street, horse-drawn vehicles were parked everywhere, and there is even a very early motorcar in the center to the right of the trolley. (Courtesy Washington County Historical Society.)

This image from around 1900 shows one of Hagerstown's open-air trolleys, used in warmer weather, turning from West Washington Street onto South Potomac Street. The square opened into a much wider open space at that time, creating an actual square, with the buildings set farther back from the road than today. The Maryland Telephone Company building is on the left, and the Central Drug Company occupied the right-hand corner. The Charles E. Shenk piano store was located just next to Central Drug.

Here is an old 1958 photograph of the southwest corner of the public square. The News Agency was next to the Professional Arts building. Next was Martha Washington Candies, the Jewel Box, Keystone Restaurant on the corner, Semler's Sporting Goods, OPO Clothes, Lobell's women's wear, and People's Drug Store. This corner of the square would be completely torn down to make room for a new, larger People's Drug Store and lunch counter. That People's store, which was on the corner, is now the Maryland Department of Assessments and Taxation. (Then image courtesy *Maryland Cracker Barrel*.)

This image shows the public square in 1923 looking up West Washington Street. Note the large traffic roundabout in the center. A great deal of the distinctive architecture of the buildings on the right of the photograph is still visible, while the left-hand side has undergone more dramatic changes. If one looks closely, the faded old lettering on the side of building announcing Eyerly's department store can still be seen.

This image of the square from around the beginning of the 20th century looks up North Potomac Street. Hagerstown's second city hall can be seen up the street. Winding the clock in the 1822 city hall was done by a line from the tower attached to a horse on the ground that pulled the clock's weights up through the tower. Construction on a third city hall began when the city received grant money from the Public Works Administration, and it is this clock tower that is seen today.

This early-20th-century view of the square faces south on Potomac Street. Roessner's Confectionery is the largest building. There is also a piano store, and next to that on the corner is the Royal Woolen Mills Company. This would all be torn down when construction was begun on the Alexander Hotel in the late 1920s. (Then image courtesy Washington County Historical Society.)

On September 25, 1957, the finishing touches were being put on the new directional signs that had just been mounted in the public square. While the sign proclaiming the location of the Hotel Alexander is gone now, the building still stands. Still in a place of honor is the historic R. Bruce Carson clock, a downtown landmark. High volumes of rail business brought prosperity to Hagerstown, and it was this that supported a number of large hotels throughout town. The sheer size of these hotels stood in testament to the importance of Hagerstown to the region.

The Blue Ridge Transportation Company's Hagerstown Bus Terminal opened on March 30, 1929, on East Washington Street. Built in cooperation with the Alexander Hotel, the terminal adjoined the hotel and had a ballroom and banquet room for the hotel on the second floor. Six coaches could fit inside to load and unload passengers simultaneously. Bus terminals were only present in 1929 in two other cities in the East—New York and Baltimore. Buses from Hagerstown ran to Baltimore and Cumberland, Maryland; Washington, D.C.; and Pittsburgh and Harrisburg, Pennsylvania, among other destinations. (Then image courtesy Washington County Historical Society.)

THE PUBLIC SQUARE BLOCKS

In 1910, the third floor of the building at 15 West Washington Street was home to St. Aldegonde and Porter Cigars. Today the building looks a little different, and the structure on the left was torn down to build People's Drug Store (now the Maryland Department of Assessments and Taxation). The building on the right is also gone; the land it occupied serves as the entrance to Hager's Row backstreet shops. (Then image courtesy *Maryland Cracker Barrel*.)

Taken on February 6, 1936, this photograph shows the Hagerstown Bank in the process of demolition on West Washington Street. Hagerstown's first bank was set up in 1807 by Nathaniel Rochester (founder of Rochester, New York). This has great importance, given that in 1810 there were only 103 banks in the entire country. The bank building pictured here was constructed in 1814. The distinctive Montgomery Ward building that went up in its place at the 1936 demolition is still easily identifiable, though it now serves as the Washington County Office Building. Note the historical plaque on the building showing the bank originally on this spot. (Then image courtesy Washington County Historical Society.)

THE PUBLIC SQUARE BLOCKS

This 1862 photograph shows the Updegraff buildings on West Washington Street. Built in the 1820s, the Updegraff factory was home to the production of hats and gloves. The factory was robbed several times during the Civil War by Confederate soldiers. Today a remnant of the past can still be viewed in the faded lettering on the top side of the building that announces Updegraff's as "clothiers, hatters, and furnishers." (Then image courtesy Washington County Historical Society.)

What was the person that took this 1920 photograph thinking? Were they taking a picture of the snowstorm or of the J. J. Newberry Company? Newberry's was located at 75 West Washington Street. Drivers have enough trouble in snow with modern cars—one has to wonder how well these early cars handled poor road conditions. The marquee to the left of Newberry's was from the Maryland Dining Room.

THE PUBLIC SQUARE BLOCKS

Benjamin Henry Latrobe, architect of the U.S. Capitol, designed the second Washington County Courthouse, shown in this image, in 1816. On December 5, 1871, a fire devastated the structure on the corner of Summit Avenue and West Washington Street. The current structure was built in 1873 and dedicated in 1874.

Here is the F. W. Woolworth Company in the Fleisher Company building on West Washington Street on April 2, 1951. Note the reflection in the store window of one of Hagerstown's old buses. A popular downtown shopping spot, Woolworth's was just one of the "five and dimes" in Hagerstown over the years. Others included McCrory's and J. J. Newberry.

This image of West Washington Street is from 1923. One of four downtown movie theaters, the Academy Theater building was originally completed in 1880 and was renovated after fire damage in 1914. Note the faded "Holly" lettering on the side of the building just past the old Academy location. This is a remnant of a department store at 74 West Washington Street. Also, note that at the time of this picture, Carson's jewelry store was located in this same building, and their landmark 1908 clock was here. It was moved to the current location in the public square in 1929.

WASHINGTON HOUSE FIRE 1879

Built in 1856, the Washington House was a thriving hotel—proclaimed the finest outside of Baltimore—on West Washington Street before a fire destroyed it in 1879. Prior to 1856, the Globe Tavern stood on this site, and George Washington is said to have stayed there when he visited Hagerstown in 1792. Next door to the Washington House is the store of W. L. Hays. The signs posted outside list "Books, Notions, Magazines, Cold Pens, Music and Bibles." The Baldwin House Hotel was built on the site after the fire and was also a well-known hostelry. The University System of Maryland at Hagerstown took over the building and now occupies this location. (Then image courtesy Washington County Historical Society.)

This is another view of West Washington Street, this time looking toward the east. While many have been repurposed, the buildings are still very recognizable. The side of one building still proclaims Eyerly's was there. The crosswalk is still in the same place but now has a traffic light. Note the buses pulled up to the side of the street on the right at the intersection with the square. Prior to the current main transfer location for the County Commuter under the railroad overpass on West Washington Street, this was one of the main transfer points in the square. Other buses stopped across the street on the southbound side of Potomac Street.

This image shows 23–25 North Potomac Street in 1916. The Hagerstown Dining Room is on the left, though it appears to be closed at the time of this photograph. On the right is Brewer and Myers, a men's clothing store. Standing from left to right are Pete Brewer, John Poffenberger, Irving Oster Jr., William Oster, Irving Oster Sr., Jake Cromer, Hobert Clopper, unidentified, John D. Myers, Frank Gray, and Carl Schlotterbeck. This structure was torn down to make way for the current downtown parking deck that occupies this site. (Then image courtesy *Maryland Cracker Barrel*.)

Hagerstown's first town hall was built around 1769 in the middle of the public square. The first floor was an open-air market. Construction began on a new town hall on June 24, 1822, at the corner of Franklin and North Potomac Streets. Hagerstown received grants from the Public Works Administration to design and build the third and current city hall in 1938. The Little Heiskell weathervane on top of city hall is a replica of the original that stood on the first and second town halls—the original is now in the Hager Museum in City Park. (Then image courtesy Washington County Historical Society.)

This old image shows 13–17 South Potomac Street, where Justus Heimel had his brewery in the late 19th century. The brewery was located on the north side of the property that would later become the site of the Maryland Theater. Heimel operated a saloon in the front of the building, a brewery was in the rear, and his houseware store was the next door on the right. Today other buildings occupy this location, but the old alley still separates the lot from the theater property.

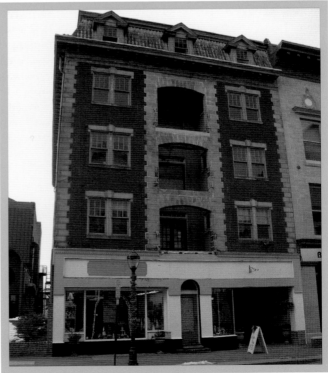

This vintage postcard shows the large Maryland Theater on South Potomac Street. Designed by noted theater architect Thomas W. Lamb, the late-Italianate-baroque-style theater opened in 1915. As the image shows, the theater originally stretched all the way up to the sidewalk in line with the other buildings on the street. A 1975 fire destroyed the entire front of the building. The theater has since been restored to its earlier glory, though it remains set back from the street.

The First Hagerstown Hose Company was
organized in 1815 and had its first home
in a shed attached to St. John's Lutheran
Church on South Potomac Street. A new
firehouse was constructed in 1881 on
the current location at 33 South Potomac
Street. A ballroom on the third floor has
been the site of many events over the years.
The character of the building was enhanced
when the marquee was added to the front
of the building in the 19th century. The
bell on the roof was purchased in 1884
and is affectionately known as "Rufus."
(Then image courtesy Washington County
Historical Society.)

THE PUBLIC SQUARE BLOCKS

When a fire broke out at the Colonial Hotel on July 1, 1947, crowds of curious people filled South Potomac Street. The Fraternal Order of Eagles (F.O.E.) was on the right side of the street, while the International Order of Red Men was across the street on the left. A restaurant still occupies the corner next to the Masonic Temple building, though it is now Shmankerl Stube. Other buildings down the street on the left were torn down when the library was constructed.

This is how the intersection of Antietam and South Potomac Streets looked in 1923. The point of view is looking north toward the public square. The Hotel Colonial building, while no longer a hotel, still looks remarkably the same from the outside, and the bell tower on the First Hagerstown Hose Company fire station can still be seen, too. The trolley tracks are long gone now, along with all the overhead wires that powered them. At that time, traffic ran in both directions on the street.

DOWNTOWN BEYOND
THE SQUARE

The Baltimore and Ohio (B&O) Railroad was one of several railroads that came into Hagerstown. In 1937, for example, over 40 steam passenger trains a day arrived in town. The lines of all the tracks stretched out from Hagerstown like wheel spokes, giving rise to Hagerstown's nickname "Hub City." The B&O Railroad was the third railway line to bring service to Hagerstown around 1861, following the Franklin Railroad in 1841 and the Cumberland Valley Railroad in 1858. This corner of Summit and Antietam Streets was one of the busiest spots in town. Today the trains are long gone, and the large *Hagerstown Herald Mail* newspaper building occupies this site. A corner of the Antietam Paper Company building still peeks out down the street, and the spire of St. John's Lutheran Church is also still visible. (Courtesy *Maryland Cracker Barrel*.)

Surrey School on Virginia Avenue was completed in 1908 and served as the boys' high school, while the girls went to Broadway School. When Hagerstown High School was opened in 1926, the boys and girls began attending coeducational classes for the first time at the new school. Surrey became an elementary school and now operates as a day care center. The Hagerstown High School building was torn down in 1980. Hagerstown broke into two high schools with the opening of North and South Hagerstown High Schools in 1956. (Then image courtesy *Maryland Cracker Barrel*.)

Surrey Public School, Hagerstown, Md.

This building on the corner of Summit and Surrey Avenues started out as the Crawford Auto Works, which was constructed by Robert Crawford originally in the stable behind his house on the corner of Surrey and Virginia Avenues. Crawford later built a larger factory around the stable as business grew. Mathias P. Moller bought out the automobile factory, and then the plant moved to a new location on Pope Avenue. Moller turned the plant into an apartment building around 1925. (Then image courtesy *Maryland Cracker Barrel*.)

Concerts in City Park have been a long-standing tradition in Hagerstown. This photograph shows the old bandstand in the park on Labor Day in 1922. The Hagerstown Municipal Band now plays in the much larger band shell that was constructed in the park in 1937–1938. The old bandstand was moved to Wheaton Park on Suman's Avenue, where it still stands today. Until 1915, Hagerstown had four city bands: the Hagerstown Concert Band, the Western Maryland Band, the South End Band, and the Silverine Band.

This early-1900s postcard is of the swans and the entrance to City Park. Note the old wooden railings and the absence of the stone wall and arched entryway that exist today. Hagerstown purchased land to create City Park in 1916, and by 1921, the swampy land had been drained and the existing lagoons deepened to create the two large lakes. Today the park is a much-loved part of downtown Hagerstown and has been called "America's Second Most Beautiful City Park" in various town informational materials over the years. The park was listed on the National Register of Historic Places in 1990.

View of Swan and Entrance to City Park

November 15, 1953, marked the ceremonies at City Park dedicating the Western Maryland Railroad's Steam Engine No. 202 to the children of Washington County. Built in 1912 by the Baldwin Locomotive Works in Philadelphia, Pennsylvania, the engine cost $19,688.92 and hauled mail, passengers, and baggage from Baltimore to Hagerstown until it was retired in 1953. The engine is underneath the large white drape in the center of the image awaiting the formal unveiling. Today the engine is just one of several train cars on display at the park.

This image shows the Washington County Museum of Fine Arts in its infancy—look how small it was! The museum was dedicated on September 16, 1931, and two wings were added to the museum in 1949, giving it the larger presence on the shore of the lake that residents are accustomed to seeing today. The museum's permanent collection is impressive and includes works from well-known artists in America as well as Europe. (Then image courtesy Washington County Historical Society.)

Jonathan Hager built his "Hager's Fancy" home, shown here prior to restoration in 1948, in 1739–1740. Hager built his frontier wilderness home to serve as a fort home and fur trading post. The walls are 22 inches thick, and the home was cleverly built to span two springs. The water bubbling up in the spring provided a protected water supply, so any poison attempts by enemies would simply be washed away in the outflow of fresh water. The home remained in private hands until the Washington County Historical Society acquired it in 1944. Today the restored home in City Park is open to the public.

Hagerstown residents turned out at the B&O station on the corner of Summit Avenue and Antietam Street in 1916 for a send-off of Company B of the National Guard as they left for Eagle Pass, Texas, to protect the United States during the Mexican border incident. The Antietam Fire Company building is behind the wagon on the train car and is still the same today. At the time, the post office was on the corner next to the fire station. The *Herald Mail* newspaper parking lot now occupies the area where the train tracks once ran. Theory has it that the fire company building was the inspiration for George Townsend's War Correspondents' Arch in Gathland State Park. (Then image courtesy Hagerstown Roundhouse Museum.)

Hagerstown's importance as a major commercial hub resulted in the construction of numerous large hotels throughout the downtown area serving the various train stations. One such hotel was the Hotel Dagmar. Built in 1911 by local organ and automobile maker Mathias P. Moller, the concrete, fireproof hotel was one of the most prestigious in the city, with light, airy rooms, hot and cold running water, and long-distance phones in each room. Today the exterior has changed little, but sadly the hotel itself has fallen into decline and is no longer the showcase it was just a century ago.

DOWNTOWN BEYOND THE SQUARE

Post Office, Hagerstown, Md.

Postmarked August 17, 1911, this postcard shows the old Hagerstown post office on the corner of Summit Avenue and Antietam Street. When Hagerstown outgrew this building, a new post office was constructed on Franklin Street in 1935–1937. The old building has remained largely the same from the exterior and now serves as the home of the Community Action Council.

This vintage image shows the old home of the Herald-Mail Publishing Company on Summit Avenue. The globe light by the doorway proclaimed that this was the *Herald Mail*. That light was later replaced with a larger sign with a clock. The newspaper moved to a new, larger home just up the street in 1980 on the previous site of the B&O Railroad Passenger Terminal, and today the old building is occupied by Mount Hope Prison Ministry. The old *Herald Mail* sign was repurposed, and the clock had the words "time to pray" added to it.

DOWNTOWN BEYOND THE SQUARE

The Washington County Free Library opened in 1901 and is the second oldest county library in the United States. Washington County also lays claim to beginning the world's first book mobile service when town librarian Mary Titcomb began sending books to rural residents on library wagons in 1904. This *c.* 1915 photograph shows one of the old book wagons parked outside the original library building at 21 Summit Avenue. The library moved to its current quarters on the corner of Antietam and South Potomac Streets in 1965. The old building is currently utilized as office space.

This old photograph shows the view looking east under the original stone Antietam Dry Bridge. Called a "dry" bridge because it did not span any water, the bridge crossed the deep ravine at Antietam Street and opened up the Southern Prospect Hill area for development. The old stone bridge was later replaced with the current structure with its graceful iron archway. (Then image courtesy Washington County Historical Society.)

Catholic missionaries began regular visits to meet the needs of area Catholics beginning in 1741, just two years after Jonathan Hager built Hager's Fancy. St. Mary's Catholic Church built its first church, a log chapel, in the late 1700s. This image is a painting of how the front of the church looked in 1826. The cornerstone of the current building was laid on July 4, 1826, and the building was completed in 1827. The vestibule and tower were added in 1870. The church and its adjacent school have continued to grow and evolve over the years. (Then image courtesy *Maryland Cracker Barrel*.)

tation C. V. R. R. & St. Mary's Catholic Church, Hagerstown, Md.

Don't expect to get home before Friday evening and maybe not this weak

This vintage postcard postmarked October 22, 1907, shows the Cumberland Valley Railroad Station on the corner of West Washington Street and Walnut Lane. St. Mary's Catholic Church can be seen across the street from the station on the opposite corner. The church is still evident today, but now Walnut Lane follows the path of the old rail tracks and the Walnut Towers senior citizen housing is located on both sides of the street where trains once click-clacked in and out of town.

This Western Maryland Railway station was completed in 1913 and served as the main rail office and housed the superintendent. In this photograph taken around 1915, the watchman is seated by his post. It was his job to stop traffic on Franklin Street when a train arrived. Today this building faces Burhans Boulevard and is the home of the Hagerstown police department. (Then image courtesy of Hagerstown Roundhouse Museum.)

Rail and road traffic often competed for the same right-of-way in downtown Hagerstown, and plans to raise the tracks over the road in the West End actually date back as far as 1910. A ground-breaking ceremony to eliminate the grade crossings between West Franklin and Church Streets finally took place on December 12, 1956. This change allowed much freer passage of traffic on the dualized U.S. Route 40 through downtown Hagerstown. Faded lettering on the R. D. McKee, Inc., building can still be discerned.

Taken in June 1988, this photograph shows the railroad yards, buildings, and roundhouse located between City Park and Burhans Boulevard in Hagerstown. Today, after a long fight to save the historic buildings, the battle was lost and the buildings are gone; all that remains are the memories of the bustling roundhouse. Concrete remnants of the roundhouse can still be seen just beyond the tracks behind the Train Room store at 360 Burhans Boulevard

Founded in 1842, the Independent Junior Fire Company met in the town hall until construction of the building on North Potomac Street began on May 11, 1852. The Juniors are now located in a new facility built on Eastern Boulevard, and the old structure is largely empty. (Then image courtesy *Maryland Cracker Barrel*.)

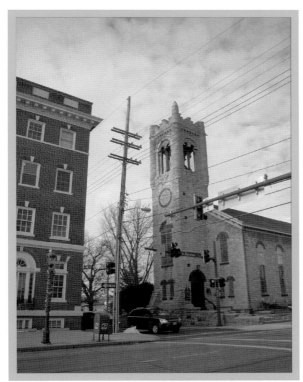

Here is a rare 1885 view of North Potomac Street and the Zion Reformed Church. Known as "Old Zion," the church is the oldest in Washington County. Founder Jonathan Hager and his wife, Elizabeth, are both buried in the adjacent cemetery. Notice that the old YMCA building did not yet exist on the corner across Church Street; the site was occupied by a home instead. The YMCA formally opened on May 1, 1922. Today the YMCA has moved to new quarters on Eastern Boulevard. (Then image courtesy *Maryland Cracker Barrel*.)

This 1905 photograph shows the new Mathias P. Moller home at 441 North Potomac Street. Moller is on the front steps holding his daughter Louise. Notice the carport on the right with a horse-drawn carriage hitched up and ready to go. The home also had a widow's walk, the railed area on the rooftop that made an excellent vantage point to look out over the city. Moller built the new house to be closer to his Prospect Street factory. (Then image courtesy *Maryland Cracker Barrel*.)

Here is how the corner of Antietam and South Potomac Streets looked in 1961, before demolition began to make room for the new Washington County Public Library. All of the buildings seen here, including the Esso gas station and Central Motors, were torn down to construct the new library. The library's former home was in the Garland Groh building on Summit Avenue. Today the library is once again bursting at the seams and is planning to expand.

St. John's Lutheran Congregation formed in Hagerstown in 1770 and constructed this Georgian-style building on South Potomac Street in 1795. The tower served as a lookout point to watch Confederate troops during the Civil War. A shed attached to the church was the first home of the First Hagerstown Hose Company before the fire company constructed their own custom quarters. (Then image courtesy Washington County Historical Society.)

Located at 205 South Potomac Street, the Elliott-Bester House is a historic structure in town. The house is the childhood home of Jesse Duncan Elliot, a U.S. naval officer and commander of American naval forces in Lake Erie during the War of 1812. The two-story home was added to the National Register of Historic Places in 1975. (Then image courtesy Washington County Historical Society.)

Located at 539 South Potomac Street, the Bester greenhouses, ice plant, and stables were a town landmark for many years. The Bester florist retail shop was located on Baltimore Street, while the greenhouses were able to spread out over on the Potomac Street site. Today Bester Florist is no longer in business, and the land across the street from Bester Elementary School is just an empty field. (Then image courtesy Washington County Historical Society.)

The corner of West Washington and Jonathan Streets was a busy location, as this June 30, 1917, image shows. Trolley tracks ran down the street, and a policeman stood in the middle of the intersection to direct the traffic. The overhead telephone wires are gone now, and traffic lights have replaced the police officer. Sovereign Bank occupies the corner where the large Hotel Maryland stood, and just visible on the left hand corner is the Nicodemus Bank building. The building still stands today and houses the Discovery Station.

Taken in December 1935 from a vantage point not far past the Prospect Street intersection, this image looks east down Washington Street toward the public square. The Hotel Alexander can be seen through the winter sky as well as the town Christmas tree mounted smack in the middle of the intersection of Washington and Potomac Streets. In those days, traffic ran in both directions on both streets, and the square functioned as a traffic roundabout instead of the one-way streets present today.

DOWNTOWN BEYOND THE SQUARE

Located at 135 West Washington Street, the Miller House dates to the 1820s. The original dwelling on the site was probably a log or wooden structure, and a brick extension was added in 1818. This extension is now believed to be the older wing at the back of the current Federal-style townhouse. This image was taken some time between 1912 and 1915. Today the house serves as a museum as well as the home of the Washington County Historical Society. (Then image courtesy *Maryland Cracker Barrel*.)

Behind the tree, the grand Georgian-style house on the left with the columns and side porches was once the home of William T. Hamilton on West Washington Street. A native of Washington County, Hamilton was elected to the U.S. Senate in 1864. He then served as governor of Maryland from 1880 to 1884. This image was taken in June 1958, before the home was torn down to make room for St. Mary's School. The photograph was taken from the vantage point of the parking lot across the street, where Mount Prospect had stood just two years earlier.

Mount Prospect, also known as the Rochester House, was built on the corner of Prospect and Washington Streets by Nathaniel Rochester in 1789. Rochester served as the first president of Hagerstown's first bank as well as postmaster, sheriff, and county court judge during his years in Hagerstown. During the Civil War, the home served as a way station for wounded. Oliver Wendell Holmes Jr. (later Supreme Court chief justice) was wounded at Antietam and brought here to be treated. The landmark home was torn down in 1956 and replaced by a parking lot. A mural painted on the lot wall depicts the home.

In the early 1920s, the Ludwig
Motor Company was located on
West Franklin Street. A close look
at the sign in the showroom window
reveals that for $825 one could buy
a brand new Pontiac. Today this
section of Franklin Street bears little
resemblance to its former self. The
Hagerstown post office now spreads
out along this site. The post office
relocated here from its former,
much smaller home on the corner
of Antietam and Summit Avenues.
(Then image courtesy *Maryland
Cracker Barrel*.)

Downtown Beyond the Square

This image shows the Hagerstown Shoe Factory, located on the corner of North Prospect and West Franklin Streets. The factory occupied both of the tall, four-story buildings. Previously one of Hagerstown's leading industries, the company began in 1911 as the Hagerstown Legging Company. In 1957, the company employed 450 skilled workers and manufactured approximately 1,450,000 shoes per year.

Chartered by the State of Maryland on April 7, 1904, Washington County Hospital opened in the former Mathias P. Moller residence on the corner of Potomac Street and Fairground Avenue on October 26, 1905. In 1912, the hospital moved to its current location on Antietam Street in the remodeled Kee-Mar College. The hospital has grown and undergone many changes in the intervening years, and now a brand new hospital is currently under construction outside the downtown area on Robinwood Drive adjacent to the Robinwood Medical Center.

When the bus terminal on East Washington Street closed down, bus service began to operate out of the new Greyhound terminal on Antietam Street. The terminal hummed with activity, and the parking area in the back was full of buses heading out to many different destinations. When Greyhound no longer required the large terminal, it moved to a small building in the back of the McDonald's on Sharpsburg Pike, not far from the Prime Outlets. Now the building sits empty, and the long, angled bus slots are deserted but still reminiscent of a busier time.

Jonathan Hager the miller, not to be confused with Jonathan Hager the founder of the town, once operated his mill at a site along what is now Mill Street and Memorial Boulevard. Daniel Stull and Nathaniel Rochester originally built the mill around 1790, and the house in Hager Park was constructed in 1791. The mill was ultimately taken over by Andrew Hager and became known as Hager's Mill. An original millstone from the mill is now embedded along with stones from other long-gone mills on the walkway outside City Park near the roundabout know as Millstone or Park Circle. Today the mill building itself is still standing on Mill Street next to Hager Park.

Hager's Mill Bridge was built by John Weaver over Antietam Creek in 1840 not far from its namesake mill. The two-arch span stood the test of time and was not replaced with the current bridge leading out Mount Aetna Road past the old Municipal Electric Light Plant until 1980. (Then image courtesy Washington County Historical Society.)

Hagerstown's first electric plant was built in 1901, but by 1928, there was a need for the larger Municipal Electric Light Plant (MELP) on Eastern Boulevard, which served the town for 44 years. The Hagerstown Light Department now has offices on Baltimore Street. At one time, the MELP was going to be brought back to life and generate power once again in conjunction with the huge recycling plant built on the corner of Eastern and Memorial Boulevards. That plant never reached its potential, though, and closed down not long after it was completed, leaving the light plant to fall into a further state of dereliction. (Then image courtesy Washington County Historical Society.)

DOWNTOWN BEYOND THE SQUARE

This photograph, taken around 1954, shows the old Winter Street School on West Franklin Street in Hagerstown's West End during demolition. The new school was being constructed at the same time the old one was coming down. The Winter Street School still serves West End elementary students today. (Then image courtesy *Maryland Cracker Barrel*.)

The Harold Kneisley Drug Store building shown in this picture has undergone some exterior changes over the years but is still quite recognizable in its location in Washington Square in downtown Hagerstown. (Then image courtesy Washington County Historical Society.)

Here is a view of Washington Square in Hagerstown from some time around 1900. Note the fountain in the center of the picture, the trolley tracks running down the brick-paved street, and the old St. Mark's Church on the "point." Western Enterprise Fire Company, incorporated in 1872, was located in their old building on the right at the time of this photograph.

This corner of Charles Street and Pennsylvania Avenue was once home to the Hagerstown Coca-Cola Bottling Works. Last owned by the Central Coca-Cola Bottling Company, the four-state region's bottler was sold to Atlanta-based Coca-Cola Enterprises, Inc., on February 28, 2006. The bottling company now has their Hagerstown operations located at a distribution center on Western Maryland Parkway. The Frederick facility was recently incorporated into the Hagerstown operations, and they brought along their 16-foot high Coke bottle that dates to the mid-1940s.

Here is a view of the fairgrounds that probably dates to the late 1800s or early 1900s. The annual fair in Hagerstown was famous throughout the eastern United States, and the major railroads that came through Hagerstown brought thousands to the fair. Trolley cars were borrowed from neighboring Frederick to help handle the huge volume of fair traffic. (Then image courtesy Washington County Historical Society.)

This is how the entrance to the Hagerstown Fairgrounds on Mulberry Avenue looked in 1907. The first fairgrounds were located along Williamsport Pike (what is now Virginia Avenue/U.S. Route 11) in the Halfway area after the Agricultural and Mechanical Association of Washington County was chartered in 1854. In 1871, the fairgrounds were located on a 14-acre plot in Hagerstown's West End, and they were moved to the current location around 1880. After almost a century, the fair closed down, and the site is now Fairgrounds Park. (Then image courtesy *Maryland Cracker Barrel*.)

CHAPTER 3

FARTHER AFIELD

One of Hagerstown's largest industries had its beginnings in an old shed on Pennsylvania Avenue. Lou and Harry Reisner joined with Ammon Kreider to form the Kreider-Reisner Aircraft Company in the late 1920s. From this unassuming start, the company became the world-famous Fairchild Aircraft Company. By 1944, Fairchild was enlarging their huge plant located at the Hagerstown Airport. One of the company's most famous planes was the C-119 Flying Boxcar, used following World War II. (Courtesy Washington County Historical Society.)

Aviation has always held a position of importance in Hagerstown, even though cars outweigh the planes in this vintage image. The City of Hagerstown Airport was dedicated on June 19, 1938, and continued to service the town's commercial flights right up until a new terminal was dedicated in 1991 on a new site across the field. Today the Washington County Regional Airport serves the entire Maryland, Pennsylvania, and West Virginia tri-state area with direct flights to Orlando on Allegiant Air and daily flights to and from Baltimore via Cape Air.

This restaurant at the airport first operated as the Always in the 1930s. Nick Giannaris purchased the establishment in 1961, and today's Airport Inn is one of Hagerstown's most well-known restaurants. Its location right next to the site where the old airport terminal was on U.S. Route 11 also makes it a popular stop-off for general aviation pilots looking for a place to eat on a weekend jaunt from other airports all around the region. (Then image courtesy *Maryland Cracker Barrel*.)

Thomas Cresap came to Maryland from England and settled in 1739 on a 500-acre land grant called Long Meadow, which was about 2 miles from what would become downtown Hagerstown. Long Meadow shopping center now resides on part of that tract of land. This image shows the empty field where the center would be as it appeared in 1957.

The 30-store shopping center opened in the spring of 1958 featuring unlimited free parking, a large supermarket, and a new Sears Roebuck store, and shopping in downtown Hagerstown would begin to change forever. Today commercial development has changed the landscape even more.

It was not many years ago that the stores in the Valley Plaza shopping center were the end of the road—there was no Sam's Club, Martin's, huge Lowe's, Staples, or any other development along Wesel Boulevard. This image shows the site during the ground-breaking for the new road linking Halfway Boulevard to Burhans Boulevard. Note how the ground was originally more elevated and had to be graded down to the current level. Mayor Steve Sager carried the flag from Wesel, Germany, Hagerstown's sister city and the road's namesake, up to the ground-breaking site. (Then image courtesy *Maryland Cracker Barrel*.)

This view of Downsville Pike in 1938 bears little resemblance to the same road today. This image was taken looking toward Hagerstown from Doubs Woods. Today Doubs Woods Park is on the right, and a shopping center is on the left. The South Hagerstown High School football field and track is just after the park on the right, while the shopping center stretches all the way to Wilson Boulevard on the left. (Then image courtesy *Maryland Cracker Barrel*.)

This country lane couldn't seem farther away from downtown Hagerstown if it tried. Yet this is how Sharpsburg Pike (South Potomac Street) looked in 1953. South Hagerstown High School, Emma K. Doub Elementary, and E. Russell Hicks Middle School had not even been constructed yet. One of the biggest changes to have taken place along Sharpsburg Pike is the huge amount of commerce that has built up around the I-70 interchanges, in particular Prime Outlets, a shopping destination that brings thousands to the area.

Wieland's Tortuga restaurant opened on the Dual Highway (U.S. Route 40) in 1948 and offered steaks and seafood as well as a cocktail bar. A 30th-anniversary advertisement in February 1978 offered coffee for 10¢, Tortuga baked pie for 30¢, and blueberry hot cakes with bacon or sausage for $1.30. The well-known landmark eatery was long associated with the Ramada Inn and is now Barefoot Bernie's at the Clarion Hotel and Conference Center. (Then image courtesy *Maryland Cracker Barrel*.)

Richardson's Snack Bar was opened along Dual Highway (U.S. Route 40) in 1948 by Evan Luther Jones. The stand was part of a national chain specializing in root beer and frozen custard. The snack bar was enclosed to allow year-round operations and began serving hamburgers, hot dogs, and fries. The restaurant was sold to Jim Resh in 1976 and was converted into Hagerstown's first buffet and salad bar. Sadly, after many years, the restaurant closed in January 2009. (Then image courtesy *Maryland Cracker Barrel.*)

The Venice Inn had its start in December 1949 when Ettore Vidoni first opened the Venice Restaurant—a lunchroom and counter in a one-story addition built on to his two-story home at the corner of Cleveland Avenue and the new Dual Highway. The first 11-room motel was built behind the house in 1950 and continued to grow. The original family home came down in 1960 to allow even more enlargement. The current multistory hotel addition opened in 1985. (Then image courtesy *Maryland Cracker Barrel*.)

Dairy Queen opened on Dual Highway (U.S. Route 40) on May 29, 1952. At the time, Towson and Salisbury were the only other Maryland towns to have similar ice cream establishments. The building may be larger now and the Dairy Queen name shortened to just DQ, but it is still a favored ice cream stop along Route 40. (Then image courtesy *Maryland Cracker Barrel*.)

This farmhouse, constructed around 1792, was the home of Revolutionary War patriot Conrad Hogmire. There is a story that a later owner was having difficulty with a fox going after his chickens. To settle the matter once and for all, he switched to dairy cows instead and wrote "Fox Deceived" on the farm. Until the day it was torn down in the late 1980s or early 1990s to make way for a new shopping center, it was known as the Fox Deceived Farm. (Then image courtesy Washington County Historical Society.)

Starland Roller Skating Rink was first built on Park Road near Pangborn around 1940. The Pangborn Corporation leased the property for storage during World War II. It reopened under new management after the war in 1946 and has been enlarged and renovated over the years. (Then image courtesy *Maryland Cracker Barrel*.)

The Pangborn Corporation was a staple industry in Hagerstown since it opened here in 1912. Everyday products such as cars and stoves must be cleaned of the residue that results from mass production, and it was the development of a process for blast cleaning that made Pangborn a success. Seven and a half acres of land across from the industrial complex was given to the city for a park in 1939. While Pangborn has now ceased production in Hagerstown, the park is still there and enjoyed by the public. (Then image courtesy *Maryland Cracker Barrel*.)

It's hard to look at the Greenberry Hills residential area now and imagine it before the houses. It was the Troup farm off Virginia Avenue from 1918 to 1948. The farmhouse itself still stands today, a large house out of sync with the smaller single family homes that now surround it. The large old barn still stands on the corner of Greenberry Road and Dogwood Drive and has been converted into apartments. (Then image courtesy *Maryland Cracker Barrel*.)

Homewood Retirement Home is a well-known staple in Williamsport, but the first Homewood was actually located outside Williamsport in Hagerstown on the corner of Virginia Avenue and Halfway Boulevard. Eleven men and women resided in this house when Homewood first opened in 1932. Today St. Joseph's Catholic Church is located on the site. (Then image courtesy *Maryland Cracker Barrel*.)

Halfway School was built in 1920, and a one-story addition was built in 1926. The school closed in 1955 and sat empty until it was torn down in August 1967. Today the Halfway Volunteer Fire Company sits on the site of the school on Lincoln Avenue. (Then image courtesy *Maryland Cracker Barrel*.)

www.arcadiapublishing.com

Discover books about the town where you grew up, the cities where your friends and families live, the town where your parents met, or even that retirement spot you've been dreaming about. Our Web site provides history lovers with exclusive deals, advanced notification about new titles, e-mail alerts of author events, and much more.

Find *Your* Place in History.